Adventures in Canadian History

THE BATTLE OF LAKE ERIE

Books for Younger Readers by Pierre Berton

The Golden Trail
The Secret World of Og

ADVENTURES IN CANADIAN HISTORY

The Capture of Detroit
The Death of Isaac Brock
Revenge of the Tribes
Canada Under Siege
The Battle of Lake Erie

Bonanza Gold
The Klondike Stampede
Trails of '98
City of Gold
Before the Gold Rush
Kings of the Klondike

Parry of the Arctic
Jane Franklin's Obsession
Dr. Kane of the Arctic Seas
Trapped in the Arctic

The Railway Pathfinders
The Men in Sheepskin Coats
A Prairie Nightmare
Steel Across the Plains

PIERRE BERTON

THE BATTLE OF LAKE ERIE

ILLUSTRATIONS BY PAUL MC CUSKER

An M&S Paperback from
McClelland & Stewart Inc.
The Canadian Publishers

An M&S Paperback Original from McClelland & Stewart Inc.

First printing April 1994

Canadian Cataloguing in Publication Data

Berton, Pierre, 1920-
The Battle of Lake Erie

(Adventures in Canadian history. The battles of the War of 1812)
"An M&S paperback original."
Includes index.
ISBN 0-7710-1424-4

1. Erie, Lake, Battle of, 1813 – Juvenile literature.
I. McCusker, Paul.   II. Title.   III. Series:
Berton, Pierre, 1920-   . Adventures in Canadian history. The battles of the War of 1812.

FC446.E1B47 1994   j971.03′4   C94-930067-5
E356.E6B47 1994

Series design by Tania Craan
Cover and text design by Stephen Kenny
Cover illustration by Scott Cameron
Interior illustrations by Paul McCusker
Maps by James Loates
Editor: Peter Carver

Typesetting by M&S, Toronto

The support of the Government of Ontario through the Ministry of Culture, Tourism and Recreation is acknowledged.

Printed and bound in Canada by Webcom Ltd.

McClelland & Stewart Inc.
The Canadian Publishers
481 University Avenue
Toronto, Ontario
M5G 2E9

1 2 3 4 5   98 97 96 95 94

CONTENTS

Map appears on page 26

The events in this book actually happened as told here. Nothing has been made up. This is a work of non-fiction and there is archival evidence for every story and, indeed, every remark made in this book.

Adventures in Canadian History

THE BATTLE OF LAKE ERIE

OVERVIEW

~

A bloody little war

WAR HAS ALWAYS BEEN a painful business. Whether you are struck by a sword, an arrow, a lance, a cannonball, a piece of shrapnel, or a bullet, it hurts dreadfully. You bleed – sometimes to death. You lose your arm or your leg. You are crippled, often for life. It has always been, and it always will be.

The War of 1812 was a minor conflict in which the United States attempted to invade Canada in order to punish Britain. It was also a bloody affair, and the lake battle described in this book was as gory a skirmish as any that took place in the larger arena of Europe. The decks of the ships that fought each other on Lake Erie on that bright September day in 1813 were slippery with the blood of seamen torn to pieces by cannon fire.

The Americans were furious because the British, locked in a life-and-death battle with Napoleon Bonaparte's France, were boarding American ships at sea and seizing every seaman born in Britain. The Americans could not attack Britain three thousand miles (4,800 km) across the water, and so they invaded the nearest British possession, Canada.

By the fall of 1813, the war had been raging for fifteen months. Three American armies had tried to invade Canada and had been hurled back. The British had seized Fort Detroit; the Americans had briefly occupied little York (Toronto) but were now hived behind the walls of Fort George on the Niagara River, the only piece of Canadian territory they occupied. The British, who had captured most of Michigan Territory, controlled Lake Erie, where the bloodiest contest of the war would soon take place.

The Americans outnumbered the British regulars by 17,000 to 7,000, but those figures don't tell us much. Many of the American "regulars" were untrained recruits, and the British had an additional two thousand Indians under the brilliant Shawnee war chief Tecumseh.

Both sides also had reserves of civilian soldiers: the militia. The American draftees, however, were called up only for short terms – as little as sixty days, as much as a year. With the exception of the Kentuckians, who loved to fight, most refused to serve beyond their term. Moreover, under the Constitution, they did not have to fight on foreign soil.

In Canada, all fit males between eighteen and sixty were obliged to serve in the Sedentary Militia. They were largely untrained and incompetent, but available in times of crisis.

The Incorporated Militia of Upper Canada was more efficient, its members having volunteered to fight for the duration of the war. Many, indeed, had joined up for patriotic reasons. In addition to the British regulars, there were also several Canadian regular units who fought as bravely and as efficiently as the British.

But these were not the neat-looking soldiers of the war paintings. On both sides, their uniforms were patched, tattered, and sometimes hanging in shreds. Shoes, tunics, and pantaloons were in short supply. There were times when the fighting men were described in official dispatches as "literally naked." Sanitation was primitive, and sickness widespread. Men sometimes went a year without being paid and hundreds deserted for that reason alone.

In battle after battle, the combatants on both sides were at least half-drunk. The doctors believed that a daily issue of spirits was essential to good health. In spite of that, the troops suffered and often died from measles, malaria, typhus, typhoid, influenza, and a variety of diseases that went under the vague names of "ague" or "lake fever."

The British were given a daily glass of strong Jamaica rum; the Americans were fed a quarter-pint (200 mL) of raw whisky. Many a farm boy got his first taste of spirits in the army, and many were corrupted by it.

The lack of hospital supplies and proper food helped to lengthen the sick list. In Canada, almost every item the army and navy needed, from rum to new uniforms, came by ship from overseas. Every scrap of canvas, every yard of rope, every anchor, cannonball, bolt, cable, and rivet came across the ocean to Montreal and was then taken by sleigh in winter or flatboat in summer to places like Fort Amherstburg. There, the British were engaged in a mad race to finish their fleet before the Americans could complete theirs and fight the battle for control of Lake Erie. When our story opens in the summer of 1813, that race was at its height.

Chapter One

~

The race to build fighting ships

ON A SOFT DAY IN MAY, 1798, a twelve-year-old English boy, Robert Barclay, takes his leave of his family to go to sea. He is a small, plump child with rosy cheeks and dark eyes which are already filled with tears. But, tears or not, he must set off by coach to join a British frigate at Greenock. He weeps bitterly as he tells an innkeeper's wife, "I am on my way to sea and will never see father, mother, brothers or sisters again."

Sixteen years later, Captain Robert Heriot Barclay is a British naval commander in charge of the flotilla being built at Amherstburg, near the present site of Windsor, Ontario. He has spent half his life in the service of the British navy, rising from the rank of midshipman at twelve, to commander at the age of twenty-eight. Now he faces his greatest trial: Canada and Britain are at war with the United States. The ships of two opposing fleets are being hammered together out of green wood on the shores of Lake Erie. It is a race against time. Soon, Barclay knows they

Robert Barclay (left) and Oliver Perry.

must face each other on these shallow, wind-blown waters. And no one can tell the outcome …

This is the story of the bloody battle that Barclay fought against his American opposite number, twenty-seven-year-old Commodore Oliver Hazard Perry. It was the only battle ever fought on any Canadian lake. We will never see another like it, because warfare has changed, ships have changed, and weapons have changed. But it makes an exciting tale, for the two fleets were evenly matched, and either side might have won.

This was the day of the sailing ship – a vessel driven solely by the uncertain wind. Thus, as Barclay and Perry both realized, they were the playthings of the weather. The wind could drive one flotilla directly into the midst of the other. If the wind was against you, however, you could only wait for the other side to attack, unless you attempted the awkward and often dangerous technique of zig-zagging across the unruly waters.

A commander was, of course, trained to manoeuvre his ship, but he was faced with a second hazard: gunfire. Cannonballs wreaked terrible havoc in those days, tearing into the rigging, causing masts to topple, sails to rip, and lines to end up in a tangled confusion.

Without sails a ship would come to a dead stop; if its rudder was smashed by enemy fire, it couldn't be steered. As more cannonballs pounded the vessel and more men were mangled, the decks would become so slippery with blood that it was difficult for the seamen to go about their duties. Ship's commanders could be killed as they walked the deck, and often enough, when the next in line took over, he was killed too, until the entire vessel was under the command of an inexperienced junior, unable to manoeuvre in the heat of battle.

The ungainly ships with their tall masts and complicated rigging might then blunder into one another and become tangled with the rigging of a sister vessel. Driven by wind and inexpertly handled, they often collided. All these things happened during the Battle of Lake Erie.

Think of it – fifteen wooden sailing ships, prisoners of the wind, most of them built on those very shores that same summer, locked in a combat that see-sawed back and forth as the cannon roared and men died, half-hidden by the smoke of battle.

It was the second year of the War of 1812, and the United States was still trying to seize Canada. In those days, travel by land was difficult and sometimes impossible. The roads weren't much more than muddy trails – where there *were* roads. The only efficient way to move about was by ship on the Great Lakes.

And so the side that controlled the lakes in this bloody, senseless war controlled the war itself.

Therefore, in the late summer of 1813, the Americans were determined to seize all of Lake Erie so they could land another invading force on Canadian soil. That touched off a frantic race to build fighting ships on those empty, forested shores, each side racing to be the first to launch an attack on the other.

The carpenters had been at work all winter building an American fleet on the shores at Presque Isle Bay in the best natural harbour on the lake.

Now, in June, the half-constructed fleet was to be increased by five small vessels that Commodore Perry had seized from the British earlier that summer.

Let us meet Perry as he tosses in his bunk aboard the captured brig *Caledonia*, in June of 1813, en route from Buffalo, New York, to Presque Isle. He is tall and well built, his plump cheeks framed by dark curly sideburns; but at the moment he is not well.

He comes from Quaker stock and the sea is bred in him, for his father was a naval captain. There are eight in the family. One older brother, Matthew, will soon go down in history as the first man to open up the mysterious island of Japan to Western commerce.

Though Perry has a quick temper, he has learned to control it, so his colleagues find him quiet, courteous, unemotional, and rather humourless. Dr. Usher Parsons, his surgeon, thinks he is the most remarkable officer he's ever known, because the seamen under him are not only fond of him, they're in awe of him. This is no narrow-minded commander. Perry is well read, plays the flute, and is a capable fencer. A student of history and drama, he is also a fearless and elegant horseman.

He has only two chinks in his armour. His main flaw is his tendency to get sick after a period of stress. The other is simpler and not much of a drawback to a man who spends his working life on the water. Perry, for reasons that have never been explained, is terrified of cows!

Perry, in his sickbed, was frustrated – as all naval commanders must have been on that squall-ridden lake – by the unpredictable weather. As he headed for Presque Isle, the wind dropped. The squadron could go no farther and so was forced to zig-zag back to its anchorage at Buffalo.

The next morning Perry tried again. His ships crawled along the shoreline, their sails drooping in a waning breeze. In the first twenty-four hours, he had moved no more than twenty-five miles (40 km).

Captain Barclay, meanwhile, was trying to guess the strength of his enemy. How many ships did the Americans have? How close were they to completing the two big brigs that would control the course of the battle? Barclay decided to send a small flotilla up the lake to try to find out.

He knew that if the Americans completed their work they would outgun him. He knew he should attack them now, but he wasn't ready. The British high command was denying him both supplies and men. Once again Barclay found himself "ill used," a phrase he had first scribbled into an old family register in his midshipman days.

His life since that time had been neither easy nor distinguished. As a run-of-the-mill officer he was no better and certainly no worse than hundreds of others. "Ill used" fits his career. He had been wounded at Trafalgar, fighting the French under Nelson. He had narrowly escaped drowning when a boat capsized. He had lost an arm in another battle, and as a result carried a combination knife and fork with which to cut up his meat, one-handed.

Officially, Barclay was only a commander, though he was called "Captain." And his was a miserable command. His crude vessel, *Detroit*, hammered together from green lumber cut on the spot and still unfinished, seemed pitiful after the great three-decked ships of the British navy.

Barclay was also painfully aware that he was second choice for the job. Another officer had turned it down because he did not want to command a badly equipped fleet in what the high command clearly viewed as a Canadian backwater. Barclay was stuck with it.

And so he did his best to figure out the odds. He sent a small flotilla to stand off the shores of Presque Isle Bay to spy on the American shipbuilders and try to discover how soon they'd be ready to fight.

Meanwhile, after a frustrating twenty-four hours spent creeping along the shoreline of Lake Erie, Perry had anchored close to the shore to escape detection. He was eager to be back at Presque Isle to oversee construction of his fleet, but he feared the enemy might be lurking about. The tension increased his illness.

A man signalled from the shore, and Perry sent a boat to bring him aboard. The news was ominous. Barclay's fleet of five vessels, led by the flagship *Queen Charlotte*, had

Building the brigantine Niagara.

appeared off Presque Isle. Perry would have to battle them before he could get into the harbour.

Sick or not, he leaped from his bunk prepared to fight. But when, on June 19, he reached his destination, Barclay's fleet had unaccountably left. They had, apparently, seen what they wanted to see and sailed off.

This was one of the strokes of good fortune that marked Perry's career. If Barclay was "ill used," Perry was blessed with good luck. The British clearly outgunned him, even without their big ship *Detroit*, still under construction at Amherstburg. The fleets would not be equal until Perry's men completed his two big brigs *Lawrence* and *Niagara*.

Barclay might easily have destroyed Perry's little flotilla as it tried to enter Presque Isle harbour, but he had no way of knowing where Perry was and left before encountering him.

The harbour, a placid sheet of water three miles (4.8 km) long and more than a mile (1.6 km) wide, was protected from the vicious storms on the lake by a six-mile (9.6 km) finger of land that curled around the outer edge. A sand bar, just six feet (1.8 m) below the surface of the lake, joined the peninsula to the far shore. That made it impossible for enemy ships to sail into the bay itself. Once Perry manoeuvred his craft over that bar the British could not get at him.

But there was one obvious disadvantage. The two big warships being built on the bay might draw too much water to clear the sand bar, especially if a British fleet was waiting outside to blast them with cannon fire as they attempted that difficult manoeuvre.

As the pilots brought their light vessels through the narrow channel, Perry's men could see the village of Erie crowding along the shoreline – some fifty frame houses, a blacksmith's shop, a tannery, and a courthouse, the last serving as a sail loft. The shipbuilders were all young, energetic men, their average age was thirty-five – and for good reason. They had to be husky, for the problems of building state-of-the-art fighting vessels hundreds of miles from a centre of civilization seemed almost insurmountable.

The only resource Presque Isle had was timber. Everything else had to be hauled in by boat and then by oxcart over roads that were no more than tracks wriggling through the forests, pocked by mud holes, blocked by stumps and deadfalls.

Perry and his troubleshooter, Daniel Dobbins, had to travel to Meadville, Pennsylvania, to scrape up steel to make axes. Iron came all the way from Bellefonte, spike rods from Buffalo, cable and hawsers from Pittsburgh, canvas from Philadelphia. There was no oakum to caulk the seams in the ships' sides; old rope had to do instead. And Dobbins had to plunder an ancient schooner for scrap iron, rigging, and shot.

Noah Brown, Perry's building superintendent, had organized an army of axemen, choppers, and sawyers, who were now stripping the surrounding forest. They worked from dawn to dusk, hacking down cucumber, oak, poplar, and ash for ribs, white pine for decks, black oak for planking and frames, red cedar and walnut for supports. This was all handwork; there were no sawmills. The race to finish the fleet before the battle began was so swift that a tree on the outskirts of the settlement could be growing one day and be part of a ship the next.

Perry's designer, a Scottish-born genius named Henry Eckford, had outfitted all the vessels brought from Black Rock and had also designed four of the six being built at Presque Isle, including the two great brigs. Because no conventional craft of their size could get across the harbour's mouth, Eckford had to design fighting vessels that had extremely shallow draughts.

It was difficult work. Food shortages caused more than one strike. Delays were maddening. Anchors ordered for the first of May had not yet arrived. In spite of that, all the ships were in the water, nearing completion.

Perry confidently expected his fleet to be ready by mid-July. But he had two problems. He didn't have enough seamen to man the ships, and he still faced the difficult task of getting his big ships across that sand bar. And now, as he looked out onto the lake, he could see that the British were again lurking, ready to tear the brigs to pieces before they could even make sail.

Chapter Two

Desperate for sailors

O N JULY 4, INDEPENDENCE DAY in the United States, the small force of British soldiers stationed at Sandwich (near present-day Windsor) could see the Americans' rockets exploding in the sky and hear the sound of church bells. The commander of the British Right Division stationed here, Major-General Henry Procter, had never felt so frustrated.

Barclay had returned from his inspection of Presque Isle full of gloom. He had seen the new American brigs already in the water, but his own ship, the huge *Detroit*, was still on land. Procter knew what he should do. He should attack at once and destroy Perry's fleet before it could be finished. Alas, he had neither men nor supplies for the job.

Nor could he expect any. The commander of the forces in Upper Canada had promised to send troops. But the troops hadn't come. Procter was convinced they never would. The British were short of gunners, clerks, servants, as well as fighting men. They were also short of food and money to pay the men. Things were so bad, Procter wrote in a letter to his commanding officer, that "we have scarcely the Means of constructing even a Blockhouse."

Captain Barclay was equally desperate for seamen. He had arrived with only a handful, and most of these were incompetent. He desperately needed three hundred trained sailors and marines to man his fleet. But his superiors wouldn't even send him a shipwright.

The problem was that the war was also being fought on Lake Ontario, where an American and a British fleet were chasing each other about without ever coming to blows. The British command wanted to hold every man and every scrap of material to meet the American threat there.

Obviously, the high command had given up on Lake Erie and was prepared to lose it to the Americans. This was part of the British strategy since the start of the war. Montreal and Quebec were to be defended at all costs, even if it meant abandoning Upper Canada (present-day Ontario) to the enemy.

The British didn't have the resources to fight everywhere. An American force was already threatening the Niagara peninsula. A thin British force held the heights at Burlington (above what is today the city of Hamilton). Another force was garrisoned at Kingston, on the St. Lawrence River. If the British weakened these strongholds by sending some of the defenders to Lake Erie, they might easily fall to the Americans.

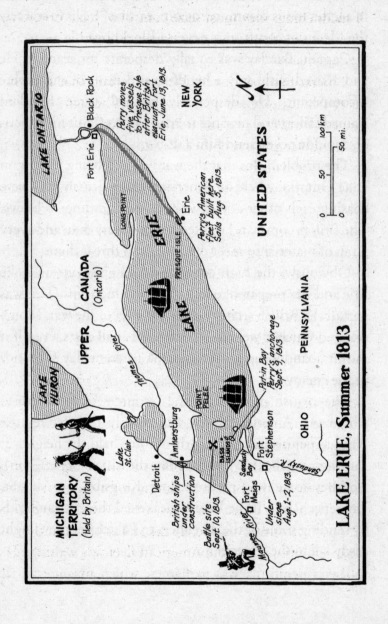

LAKE ERIE, Summer 1813

And so the orders to Procter and Barclay were simple, if maddening: they must seize control of Lake Erie. Once they did that the British would have no trouble protecting Lake Ontario.

Procter felt abandoned. He was certain that if he had received the promised men and supplies he could have destroyed all of Perry's vessels at Presque Isle. That would have given him command of the lake and acted as a diversion to protect the British.

The American fleet was rapidly approaching fighting trim. When Barclay's new ship, *Detroit*, and two gunboats being built at Amherstburg were finished, the odds would again be even. But Barclay knew the *Detroit* would not be in the water until July 20. After that she would have to be rigged with masts and sails.

The British faced even more difficulties than Perry when it came to building warships. Canada had no steel or iron mills, no Pittsburghs or Philadelphias, and no manufacturing worthy of the name. Everything except timber – nails, bolts, pulleys, lead, copper, glass, paint, resin, cordage, sails – had to come from Montreal and Quebec and, ultimately, from England.

The cannon Barclay had ordered for the big ship were taken over by the British at Kingston for other purposes. Now he had to order new guns, which would have to be shipped across the Atlantic, up the St. Lawrence, and across Lake Ontario, where the American fleet was waiting. The Niagara peninsula was in flames, which meant that the guns would have to be transported by a long land route through the forests of Upper Canada to Amherstburg.

That spring, when the Americans had attacked York (Toronto), the British had lost fifty thousand dollars' worth of stores – guns, ammunition, cables, cordage, canvas, tools – all destined for Barclay's fleet. When he'd asked his superiors for more he had been told to get it by fighting the Americans.

But Barclay knew his force wasn't strong enough to attack the Americans. Presque Isle was too well guarded. Meanwhile, General Procter's Indian allies were becoming restless. Supplies were so short they were existing on bread. And the traditional presents, which the military always distributed, hadn't arrived.

Procter knew he must do something. The Indians needed the excitement of a battle. If they didn't get it they would drift away to their villages, and the army would be terribly weakened. For, in this strange war, the Indians were a key force.

Tecumseh, the great Shawnee war chief, who hated the Americans, was Procter's chief Native ally. He was eager to mount an attack on Fort Meigs, the American stronghold on the Maumee River, just south of Lake Erie. This was the headquarters of the American commander, William Henry Harrison, a future U.S. president. Procter was convinced that Harrison's stronghold was too tough a nut to crack, but he had no choice: if he didn't go on the attack he would lose his Indian allies.

He set off with an army of five thousand, placed his troops on the right bank of the river, and planned an ambush. It failed.

The Americans drove the British back, but that didn't really bother Tecumseh. He and his people were still full of fight, and the Shawnee was convinced that Fort Stephenson, a more lightly held bastion, could easily be taken. Again, Procter had no choice but to follow Tecumseh's lead.

Fort Stephenson lay a mile or so upriver from Sandusky Bay on the south shore of Lake Erie. With its weak garrison of one hundred and fifty soldiers and its huddle of wooden buildings, it certainly couldn't be held against an army of five thousand. Harrison realized that.

But now an incredible incident took place. Harrison sent an order to the fort's young commander, Major George Croghan, to set the fort on fire and get out. But Croghan pretended he hadn't understood! When the British gunboats swept up Sandusky Bay propelled by a spanking breeze, Croghan held his ground.

Procter had Croghan outgunned. He had six-pounders (2.7 kg) to destroy the palisades, and howitzers to lob more cannonballs over the walls to maim the defenders inside. All Croghan had was one ancient six-pounder, left over from the Revolution, known as "Old Betsey."

Procter's force outnumbered Croghan's by at least seven to one. But in battle it is not always the largest force that wins, but the character of the fighting men.

Neither side expected victory in this strange contest.

Harrison looked at the odds and was prepared to give up. Croghan, however, had no intention of withdrawing. Procter, on the other hand, didn't believe the fort could be taken; but with Tecumseh pushing him he had no course but to attack.

Procter felt his command slipping away. Droves of his Native allies had already deserted because of the failure to grab Fort Meigs. So Procter now planned a two-pronged attack, with the British regulars storming the fort from one side, the Indians from the other.

The British mount a costly assault on Fort Stephenson.

Croghan had only one thing on his side: the will to win. Procter was within two hundred and fifty yards (230 m) of the fort by dawn, August 1. That day he hurled five hundred cannonballs and shells at the Americans. He planned a fake attack at the south end to deceive the defenders, but Croghan was prepared for that. He was convinced, rightly, that the real attack would come from the northwest.

The British began the assault at four that afternoon. But Procter was a flawed commander. He tended to panic when steadfastness was required. His men were ill-prepared.

They had no scaling ladders to launch against the sixteen-foot (5 m) palisade and their axes were dulled from weeks of misuse.

A deep ditch encircled the fort. The British reached a point twenty paces from this obstacle and formed themselves in line for a frontal assault – the most difficult and dangerous of all military manoeuvres.

At that point Croghan's Kentucky sharpshooters opened up. The palisade was higher and the ditch deeper than the attackers had expected. Soon the ditch was clogged with dead and dying men, struck down as they attempted vainly to breach the double obstacle.

When darkness fell, a rising moon cast a pale light on the carnage. In the ditch and the ravine beyond, men were groaning, dying, and cursing Procter for deserting them.

The assault had been a failure. The General had been bested by a youth who had just passed his twenty-first year. It did not bode well for the battle that was looming on the grey waters of the lake.

Chapter Three

❧

Perry's luck

O N AUGUST 1, WHEN THE BRITISH mounted their flawed attack on Fort Stephenson, Oliver Hazard Perry rose at last from his sickbed. He had had another stroke of good fortune – "Perry's Luck," it would come to be called. He learned that the British fleet, which had been hovering just outside the bay for almost two weeks, had vanished.

The blockade was ended. His own ships were now ready to sail. The moment had come to get them across the sand bar that blocked the entrance. So Perry shook off the "bilious" fever that seemed to strike him after long periods of stress and fatigue.

These had not been easy weeks. He still didn't have enough experienced seamen or officers to man his ships. He was mortified that he couldn't give naval help to Harrison during the siege of Fort Meigs. The high command had only sent him a handful of men, the dregs of the fleet: "a motley set, blacks, soldiers and boys," in Perry's description. But he was eager to attack Barclay, even with ships that were partially manned. "I long to have at him," he declared.

A second detachment of sixty men arrived, but these weren't much use to Perry. Most were worn down by disease; one-fifth was suffering from fever and dysentery.

Two hundred soldiers had accompanied him from Black Rock, but these had long since been ordered back to Lake Ontario. His only defence force was a comic opera regiment of Pennsylvania militia, too afraid of the dark to stand watch at night. Perry demanded to know why they weren't at their posts and received a jarring comment from their commander.

"I told the boys to go, Captain," he said, "but the boys won't go."

Perry wasn't worried about Procter, who was wary now of attacking *any* defensive position. Perry didn't contemplate defence – he was determined to attack. His force, at that moment, was clearly superior to Barclay's, because the British brig *Detroit* remained unfinished.

"What a golden opportunity if we had men," Perry wrote. Yet, because he didn't have enough, he was "obliged to bite [his] fingers in vexation." Fortunately, the enemy was out of the way for the moment. He could at last get his ships into the open lake without fear of attack. Or were the British faking? Perhaps; but he intended to try anyway.

Now he suffered a new frustration. The water had dropped to a depth of only four feet (1.2 m) at the sand bar.

The two brigs, *Lawrence* and *Niagara*, drew nine feet (2.7 m). That meant they were trapped.

Luckily, Noah Brown had foreseen just such a calamity. His solution was ingenious. He built four huge box-like scows, known as "camels." These could be floated or sunk at will. By placing a camel on either side of a ship and sinking both camels below the surface, the vessel could be raised up by means of ropes and windlasses. Then it was set on a series of wooden beams resting on the camels. The scows were then plugged, pumped out, and brought to the surface. With the big ship resting on the supports, the entire ungainly contraption could be floated easily across the bar.

But that wasn't easy. Before the big brigs could be raised up on the camels, the smaller vessels in the fleet had to be lightened and hauled across the sand bar to act as a protective screen in case the British squadron should reappear. More guns were needed to meet that threat. And so the brig *Niagara* was brought up close to the bar to act as a floating battery. If the British returned, she would fire broadside at the advancing ships.

Now *Niagara*'s twin, *Lawrence*, a fully rigged brig, pierced for twenty guns, was hauled forward. For three hours the sweating seamen stripped her of her armaments. The camels were brought alongside and the brig was hoisted two feet (.6m). It wasn't enough; she still drew too much water. The process had to be repeated. It wasn't until mid-morning, August 4, that she was finally floated free.

The officers and men had spent two sleepless nights, but the work still wasn't over. Now *Lawrence* had to be refitted – a task that took them until midnight. And then *Niagara* had to be floated over the bar, protected by *Lawrence's* guns. Could they get the ships out of the harbour before the British returned? Alas, before *Niagara* could be freed of the bar, two sails were seen through the haze on the horizon. Barclay was back.

Again Perry's luck held. Barclay simply could not believe that Perry could get those two big ships over the bar. The British commander was elated at the prospect of treating them as sitting ducks. Barclay had gone off to attend a dinner in his honour at Port Dover. There, in reply to a toast, he announced he expected to return "to find the Yankee brigs hard and fast aground on the bar at Erie ... in which predicament it would be but a small job to destroy them."

Now, nature helped to deceive the British. The wind cast such a haze across the mouth of the bay that Barclay thought that Perry had somehow got his whole fleet over the bar and into the open lake. Perry sent two of his smaller vessels out to the lake to fire a few shots, and Barclay, believing himself outgunned, retired. He did not yet have his big ship *Detroit* in fighting trim. But it wasn't until midnight, August 5, that Perry's fleet of ten ships, all fully armed, headed out into the lake for a two-day trial run, vainly seeking the elusive British.

Perry's worries still weren't over. The trouble was that many of the men serving under him were volunteers, and, under the terms of their enlistment, ready to go home. He had to pay them off and was left only with those men who had signed up for four months' service. Thus, he had less than half the men he needed to man his fleet. Of these, less than a quarter were regular naval personnel. As for his officers, they had little experience. Perry realized that delay was dangerous, but he knew that he wasn't yet prepared to face the enemy.

He was still suffering from fatigue and fever. The struggle to get the *Lawrence* over the bar had worn him down. For two days he had gone without food or sleep. He had also received a taunting letter from his superior officer on Lake Ontario, Admiral Chauncey. The sensitive Perry decided to quit. He told the Secretary of the Navy that he could not "serve longer under an officer who has been so totally regardless of my feelings." But the dispute was patched up, and to Perry's delight he got his reinforcements – several officers and eighty-nine seamen under Jesse Elliott.

As events would prove, Elliott was a bit of a problem. Though junior in rank to Perry, he was far better known to the American public – a national hero because he had led a daring raid against the British the previous summer, the only victory in a string of scandalous defeats. He was four years older than Perry, and at one time had been picked to command the U.S. naval force on Lake Erie – until Perry overtook him. He was vain, boastful, and not always generous with subordinates, for he liked to get credit for any victory. He was also a bit of a troublemaker, having already fought one duel. Perry, however, was glad to see him when he arrived on August 10.

The men Elliott brought were better than the previous seamen. Perry, whose flagship would be *Lawrence*, gave Elliott command of *Niagara* and allowed him to choose his own crew. The ambitious Elliott grabbed the pick of the crop. *Lawrence*'s sailing master complained that the vessels now were unequally manned, the best men having been taken for *Niagara*. But Perry was so happy to see them that he overlooked Elliott's rudeness.

He was far more concerned about the big British ship *Detroit*, now nearing completion at Amherstburg. It was larger than any of his own vessels, and so he took care to cruise the lake ready for battle.

Since he only had forty men who knew anything about guns, he started to drill his force. His plan was to force Barclay out of his harbour at Amherstburg and, if that failed, to transport General Harrison's army across the lake to attack Procter. Meanwhile, he took his fleet into Put-in Bay, a safe anchorage not far from Sandusky Bay, at the western end of the lake.

There, sickness struck once more. Perry fell dangerously ill again with fever. His thirteen-year-old brother, Alexander, was also sick. The chief surgeon was too ill to work. His assistant, also ill and flat on his back on a cot, had to be carried from ship to ship to minister to the sick.

On August 31, more reinforcements arrived: one hundred Kentucky riflemen. Their job was to act as marines and sharpshooters in the battle to come. Most had never seen a ship before and couldn't hide their astonishment or curiosity. They climbed the masts, plunged into the holds, trotted about each vessel from sick bay to captain's cabin, exclaiming over the smallest details.

The next day Perry was well enough to put his squadron in motion towards Amherstburg, hovering outside the harbour just as Barclay had once blockaded him. He could see *Detroit* was now fully rigged. But Barclay declined to come out.

A few days later, three escaped prisoners from Amherstburg warned him that Barclay was preparing for battle. Perry now had a pretty good idea of his adversary's strength, but he overestimated Barclay's manpower, which was in fact no greater than his own. Actually, in fire power Perry now outgunned Barclay two to one.

Again sickness struck him. In spite of this, he called a council in his cabin. Of his 490 men, he learned, almost a quarter were ill, and all three surgeons were now sick. Some of the invalids, however, would still be able to fight.

Here, each commander was given his instructions. Perry, in *Lawrence*, would attack Barclay's flagship, *Detroit*. Elliott, in *Niagara*, would attack the next largest vessel, *Queen Charlotte*. And so on down the line.

British and American tactics in the battle to come would

depend on the kind of guns with which each ship was equipped. The Americans preferred short, stubby, powerful guns called "carronades." The British favoured long guns that could pound the American ships from a distance.

With his carronades Perry would be forced to fight at very close quarters. Unless he could get close to the British and hammer them hard, the British, with their longer range, could batter him to pieces while he could not reply.

He left nothing to chance. He had already worked out a series of signals for the day of action. Now he handed every officer written instructions, telling them to make sure they engaged their opposite number in close action at half cable's length (91 m). Those long guns bothered him. If he had his way, his powerful short-range carronades would batter Barclay's at point-blank range.

As the officers rose to leave, Perry called them back and went over the plan again. He wanted to make absolutely sure they would bring the British fleet into close action. When he dismissed them he echoed a phrase of Horatio Nelson's: "If you lay the enemy close alongside you cannot be out of your place."

But that still wasn't enough for Perry. He stood on the deck and repeated Nelson's phrase. He couldn't get those long British guns out of his mind. Barclay, he knew, could easily stand out of range, especially if the wind was right, and reduce his fleet to matchwood before a single American shot could strike him.

It was ten o'clock on a lovely September evening. The

moon was full, the lake like black glass tinselled with silver. From the shore came the hum of voices around campfires, and the *peep-peep* of frogs in nearby Squaw Harbour. From the quarterdecks of the anchored vessels, the low murmur of officers could be heard, discussing the coming battle, and also the crackle of laughter – sailors telling jokes.

Perry went to his cabin. He had letters to write. If the battle should come and he was victorious, they wouldn't have to be sent. But if he should fall and die, these would be his final messages.

Chapter Four

The eve of battle

IN AMHERSTBURG THAT FATEFUL September 9, Robert Heriot Barclay knew that he must lead his squadron into Lake Erie and fight the Americans – he had no other choice. He realized the odds were against him and that only a miracle could bring him victory. But Amherstburg was on the verge of starvation. His own crews were on half-rations. They didn't even have a barrel of flour left.

Procter's fourteen thousand followers, mostly Indians with wives and children, had been reduced to a few barrels of pork, some cattle, and a little unground wheat. Barclay held off until the last moment, hoping for the promised reinforcements, guns, and equipment for his new ship, *Detroit*. Now he could hold out no longer. He must attempt to run down the lake to bring provisions from Long Point, on the northern shore of Lake Erie. He also knew that Perry's fleet was waiting to intercept him at Put-in Bay, thirty miles (48 km) to the southeast. Perhaps he could get past Perry unseen, though that seemed unlikely. But he did not intend to shirk the encounter.

Like Perry, he was badly undermanned. Indeed, he was in far worse condition than his adversary. His officers didn't know their own men. The men didn't know their ships. Barclay had been pleading for weeks for reinforcements, but the merest handful had arrived, most of them untrained.

The troops had not been paid for months. The civilian workers had refused to work on the ships without wages. Procter had warned the high command that "there are not in the Fleet more than four and twenty *seamen*." Barclay had echoed these remarks to his own command.

"If you saw my Canadians, you would condemn every one … as a poor devil not worth his Salt."

All the Canadian Governor General, George Prevost, could do was write foolish letters likely to infuriate both commanders. The Governor General had reached the Niagara frontier on August 22 and ignored all his subordinates' worries. He said that the situation "may be one of some difficulty," but "you cannot fail in honourably surmounting it" – as if mere words could win a battle!

"Captain Barclay … has only to dare, and the enemy is discomfited," he said. The Governor General was a prisoner of his own optimism.

Prevost wrote glibly of seamen "valorous and well disciplined." Procter replied, "Except, I believe, the 25 Captain Barclay brought with him, there are none of that description on this lake."

Barclay was also short of guns and equipment because of

the American attack on York that spring (see *Canada Under Siege* in this series). To outfit his new ship he had to borrow a weird collection of cannon from the ramparts of Fort Amherstburg. The big guns came in half a dozen sizes. Each needed separate ammunition. That meant that confusion would reign among the untrained gunners in the heat of battle.

The guns could not be fired efficiently. The matches and tubes were spoiled or corroded. To fire a gun, an officer had to snap his flint-lock pistol over the touch-hole – an awkward procedure that slowed the rate of fire. Indeed, everything on *Detroit* was makeshift. Some of the sails, cables, and blocks had been borrowed from *Queen Charlotte* and other vessels, there being no others available in Amherstburg.

The Governor General kept promising that more guns and men were on their way. On September 1, the British landed a dozen twenty-four-pound (11 kg) carronades at Burlington, on Lake Ontario. But the guns got no farther. A few more reinforcements did arrive – two lieutenants, two gunners, and forty-five seamen who turned out to be, in Barclay's opinion, "totally inadequate." Sixteen were mere boys.

Prevost assured him that more were on the way, but Barclay couldn't wait. At ten o'clock on that calm, moonlit night, as Perry paced his own deck a few leagues away, Barclay's fleet of six warships slipped their moorings and moved out into the Detroit River onto the shining waters of the shallow lake.

In Europe, the noose was tightening around Napoleon. Austria had joined the Allied cause. The Prussians had already dealt the French a stunning setback at Katzbach. In St. Petersburg, Russia, three distinguished American diplomats were attempting peace talks with Britain, with the Tsar acting as mediator. But none of this could have the slightest effect on the contest being waged here on a silent lake in the heart of a continental wilderness.

And so, here is Barclay, walking the quarterdeck of his untried ship. What is he thinking? Certainly he has looked at the odds, which are against him. Perry has ten vessels – three brigs, six schooners, and a sloop. Barclay has six – two ships, a brig, two schooners, and a sloop. Ships and brigs are square rigged, the former with three masts, the latter with two. It is largely on these big vessels that the contest will depend.

Barclay's flagship, *Detroit*, was the largest vessel on the lake. It was 126 feet (38 m) long, at least fifteen feet (4.6 m) longer than either of Perry's two brigs. But firepower counts more than size, and here Perry had the advantage, especially at close quarters. Long guns were most effective at eight hundred yards (732 m). At three hundred (274 m), the stubby carronade could do greater damage. Perry's could shatter the British fleet with a combined broadside weighing a total of 664 pounds (299 kg). The British, who

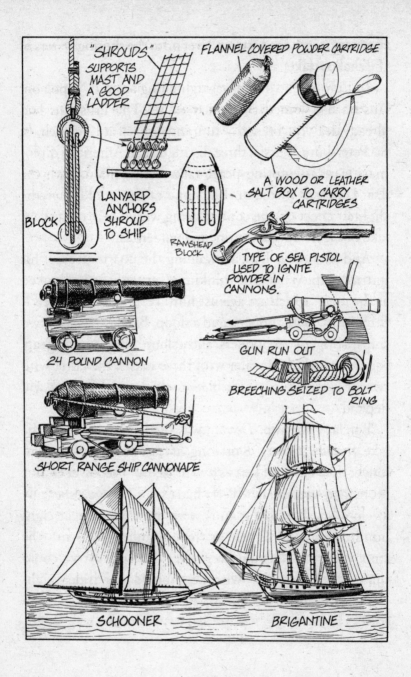

"SHROUDS." SUPPORTS MAST AND A GOOD LADDER

FLANNEL COVERED POWDER CARTRIDGE

A WOOD OR LEATHER SALT BOX TO CARRY CARTRIDGES

BLOCK

LANYARD ANCHORS SHROUD TO SHIP

RAMSHEAD BLOCK

TYPE OF SEA PISTOL USED TO IGNITE POWDER IN CANNONS.

24 POUND CANNON

GUN RUN OUT

BREECHING SEIZED TO BOLT RING

SHORT RANGE SHIP CANNONADE

SCHOONER

BRIGANTINE

preferred the longer range, could hurl only 264 pounds (119 kg) of metal at the enemy.

Barclay was also short of trained gunners and seamen. Of his total crew of 440, at least 300 were soldiers, not sailors. But three of every five men in Perry's crews were seamen.

Barclay had one advantage only. Perry's two largest vessels, *Lawrence* and *Niagara*, were inferior to him in long-range firepower. At long range the American flagship faced nine times its own firepower. No wonder Perry was desperate to fight at close quarters.

Barclay had a pretty good idea of the two fleets' comparative strength. He had looked over the opposing squadron off Amherstburg, climbing to the highest house in the village to examine the vessels through his glass. His strategy was the opposite of Perry's. He intended to use his long guns to batter the Americans before they could get within range with their stubby carronades.

But here both men were faced with the limitations of wooden sailing ships. A great deal depended on forces over which neither man had any control. If Barclay had the "weather gauge" – that is, if the wind was behind him so that he could manoeuvre his ships easily – then Perry would be in trouble. But if Perry had the gauge, the wind would drive him directly into the heart of the British fleet and allow him to use his short-range weapons.

For both men, the next day would tell the tale. For all Barclay knew, it might be his last day on earth – as it might be Perry's. He might emerge a hero, honoured, promoted, decorated. More likely, he thought, he would have to shoulder the blame for defeat.

How would fate, fortune, wind, and circumstance use him in the approaching battle? The next day would tell.

Chapter Five

~

Launching the attack

I T WAS SUNRISE, September 10, at Put-in Bay. Perry's lookout, high up on the mast of *Lawrence*, spotted a distant silhouette beyond the cluster of islands.

"Sail, ho!" he cried.

In an instant Perry leaped from his bunk. The cry seemed to act as a tonic to his fever. Up the masthead went his signal: *Get under way.* Within fifteen minutes his men had hauled in sixty fathoms (110 m) of cable, hoisted anchors, raised the sails, and steered the nine vessels for a gap between the islands that shielded the harbour.

The wind was against Perry. He could gain the weather gauge only by beating around to the windward of some of the islands. That would require much time, and Perry was impatient to fight.

"Run to the lee side," he told his sailing master, William Taylor.

"Then you will have to engage the enemy to leeward, sir," Taylor reminded him. That would give the British the advantage of the wind.

"I don't care," said Perry. "To windward or leeward, they will fight today." So off they went.

The fleet was abustle. Decks had to be cleared for action so that nothing would get in the way of the recoil of the guns. Seamen were hammering in flints, lighting rope matches, placing shot in racks or in coils of rope next to the guns. Besides round shot, to pierce the enemy ships, the gunners would also fire canister – a menacing cluster of iron balls encased in a tin covering – or grapeshot, a similar collection arranged around a central core in a canvas or quilted bag.

Perry's favourite black spaniel ran about the deck in excitement until his master ordered him confined in a china closet where he would no longer be underfoot. Then he collected the ship's papers and signals in a weighted bag, which could be thrown overboard in the case of surrender, denying that information to the enemy. At the same time his men were getting out stacks of pikes and cutlasses to push back the British if they attempted to board the ship. In addition, they sprinkled sand on the decks to prevent slipping when the blood began to flow.

The assistant surgeon, Usher Parsons, was setting up a makeshift hospital in *Lawrence's* wardroom. The brig was so shallow that there wasn't any secure place for the wounded. They would have to be kept in a ten-foot (3 m) square patch of floor, level with the water line – as much at the mercy of the British cannonballs as were the men on deck above.

Suddenly, just before ten, the wind shifted to the south-east – Perry's Luck! The Commodore now had his weather gauge. Slipping past Rattlesnake Island, he bore down on the British fleet, five miles (8 km) away.

Barclay had turned his ships into the southwest. The sun bathed his line of vessels in a soft morning glow, shining on the spanking new paint, the red ensigns, and the white sails against the cloudless sky. Perry picked up a glass and stared at the British fleet. He realized that Barclay's line of battle wasn't what he had expected. The small schooner *Chippawa*, armed with a single long gun at the bow, was at the head of the line. Behind it was a big three-master, which must certainly be *Detroit*. Perry had thought the British lead vessel would be the seventeen-gun *Queen Charlotte*, designated as Elliott's target.

As a result of this new information, Perry had to change his battle order to bring his heaviest vessels against those of the enemy. The ambitious Elliott, up ahead in *Niagara*, had originally asked to be in the forefront, but now he was moved farther back, much to his chagrin. Perry himself intended to take on Barclay. Two American gunboats would operate off his bow to act as dispatch vessels. *Caledonia* would engage the British brig *Hunter*, and Elliott in *Niagara* would follow to take on the larger *Queen Charlotte*. Four smaller vessels would bring up the rear – nine ships in all. (The sloop did not take part.)

All hands were piped to quarters. Tubs of rations, bread bags, and the standard issue of grog were on hand for the battle. Perry produced a flag he had had prepared for the moment with the words "Don't give up the ship!" embroidered on it.

"Shall I hoist it?" he asked. A cheer went up. Even the sick – those who could walk – came out as Perry, moving from battery to battery, examined each gun, murmured words of encouragement, exchanged a joke or two with the Kentuckians he knew best, and saved his special greeting for men from his home state of Rhode Island.

"Ah, here are the Newport boys! *They* will do their duty, I warrant!"

To a group of old hands, who had experience of earlier contests and had removed their cumbersome headgear and tied handkerchiefs around their foreheads, he said, "I need not say anything to you: *you* know how to beat those fellows."

Now a silence descended on the lake. The British line, closed up tight, waited motionless in the light breeze. The American squadron, with the breeze behind it, approached at an angle of fifteen degrees. The hush was deadly. To David Bunnell, a seaman aboard *Lawrence*, it resembled "the awful silence that precedes an earthquake." Bunnell had been at sea a long time and had served in both navies, but now he found his heart beating wildly as all nature seemed "wrapped in awful suspense."

In the wardroom below, its single hatch closed tight, the only surgeon available, Usher Parsons, sat in the half-light, unable to shake from his mind the horrors he knew would follow.

At the guns, the men murmured to each other, giving instructions to comrades in case they should fall, relaying messages to wives and sweethearts. Perry, in his cabin, reread his wife's letters, then tore them to shreds so the enemy wouldn't get them. "This is the most important day of my life," he said quietly.

Slowly the distance between the two fleets narrowed. Minutes dragged by. Both sides held their breath. Perry had little control over the speed of his vessels. At their rear, the slower gunboats were already lagging badly behind.

Soon only a mile (1.6 km) separated the two big flagships. Suddenly a British bugle broke the silence, followed by cheers from Barclay's fleet. A cannon exploded. The sound seemed electrifying. A twenty-four-pound (11 kg) ball splashed into the water ahead. The British were still out of range. But the battle had begun.

Chapter Six

The strange behaviour of Jesse Elliott

SLOWLY THE AMERICAN FLEET SLIPPED forward under the light breeze. Five minutes went by, and then another explosion. A cannonball tore its way through *Lawrence's* bulwarks. A seaman fell dead, killed by a flying splinter. The British had found their range. "Steady, boys, steady," said Perry.

Up from below came an odd whimpering and howling – Perry's spaniel. The cannonball had torn its way through the planking of the china closet, knocking down all the dishes and terrifying the animal, who would continue to bark throughout the course of the battle.

Perry called out to his first lieutenant, John Yarnell, to hail the little *Scorpion*, off his windward bow, by trumpet. He wanted her to open up on the British with the only long gun she had. He ordered his own gunners to fire *Lawrence's* long twelves, but with no effect, for the British were still out of range.

Now Barclay's strategy became apparent. He had decided to ignore all the other vessels in Perry's fleet and have his ships concentrate their combined fire, a total of thirty-four guns, on *Lawrence*. He intended to batter Perry's flagship to pieces before she could get into range, then attack the others.

The British vessels formed a tight line, no more than a hundred yards (91 m) apart. At this point Perry's superior numbers didn't count for much. As he pulled abreast of the British, his gunboats were too far in the rear to do any damage. He signalled all his vessels to close up and for each to engage her chosen opponent. Finally, at twelve-fifteen, he brought *Lawrence* into carronade range of *Detroit* – so close that the British believed he was about to board their ship.

As the thirty-two-pound (14.5 kg) canisters sprayed the decks of his flagship, Robert Barclay suffered a serious stroke of bad luck. His seasoned second-in-command, Captain Finnis, in charge of *Queen Charlotte*, had been unable to reach his designated opponent, partly because the wind had dropped and partly because Elliott, in *Niagara*, had remained out of range. So Finnis, under heavy fire from the American *Caledonia*, determined to move up the British line ahead of *Hunter* and punish *Lawrence* at close quarters with a broadside from his carronades.

But just as his ship shifted position, Finnis was felled by a cannonball and died instantly. His first officer died with him, and a few minutes later the ship's second officer was knocked senseless by a shell splinter.

And so, at twelve-thirty, *Queen Charlotte*, the second most powerful ship in the British squadron, fell under the

The American fleet approaches Barclay's flagship.

command of a young inexperienced lieutenant in the Provincial Marine, Robert Irvine. He was no replacement for the expert Finnis, and all he had to support him was a master's mate of the Royal Navy, two boy midshipmen from his own service, a gunner, and bo'sun. Barclay had lost his main support.

Despite that, *Lawrence* was reeling under the British hammer blows. The tumult aboard the American flagship was appalling. Above the shrieks of the wounded and the dying and the rumblings of the gun carriages came the explosion of cannon and the crash of round shot splintering masts, tearing through bulwarks, ripping guns from their carriages.

The decks were soon a rubble of broken spars, tangled rigging, shredded sails, and dying men. And over the whole scene hung a thick pall of smoke, blotting out the sun and turning the bright September noon to gloomy twilight.

Here now was the true horror of naval warfare. Lieutenant John Brooks, the head of Perry's marines, the handsomest officer at sea this day, turned, smiling, to pass a remark to Perry, when a cannonball tore into his hip, ripped off a leg, and hurled him to the deck. In terrible agony, Brooks screamed for a pistol to end his life. Perry ordered the marines to take him below.

As they bent over him, Brooks's young black servant, just twelve years old, bringing cartridges to a nearby gun, saw his fallen master and flung himself, sobbing, to the deck.

Usher Parsons could do nothing for Brooks. He had only a few hours to live.

Parry's first lieutenant, John Yarnell, presented a grotesque appearance. His nose, perforated by a splinter, had swollen to twice its normal size. Blood from a scalp wound threatened to blind him, but Parsons bound it up with a bandanna and Yarnell went back to the deck.

At that point he walked into a cloud of cattail down, torn from a pile of hammocks by a cannonball. Wounded a third time, he came below once more for medical help, his bloody face covered with down, looking like a gigantic owl. At this bizarre spectacle, the wounded men couldn't help laughing. "The devil has come for us!" they cried.

Perry himself seemed to bear a charmed life. Men were dropping all around him, but he didn't suffer a scratch. As Perry stopped to give aid to one of his veteran gun captains, the man, drawing himself up, was torn in two by a twenty-four-pound (11 kg) cannonball.

Perry's second lieutenant, Dulaney Forrest, was standing close to him when a shower of grapeshot struck Forrest in the chest, knocking him to the deck. But the shot was spent. Perry asked him if he was badly hurt, whereupon the stunned officer, regaining consciousness, cried out, "I'm not hurt, sir, but this is my shot!" and he pulled out a handful from his waistcoat and pocketed it as a souvenir.

Perry's little brother, Alexander, acting as a messenger during the din of battle, was also knocked senseless by a splinter, though otherwise unhurt – and still the Commodore remained untouched. For the next century, American naval men would speak in awe of Perry's Luck. Luck … mingled with good sense. Unlike Nelson, who stood on the decks at Trafalgar in a glittering full-dress uniform, an easy target for the enemy, Perry had donned the plain blue jacket of a common sailor.

By one-thirty, *Lawrence*'s sails were so badly shredded that the brig could no longer be controlled. In spite of the sand, the decks were slippery with blood, which seeped through the seams and dripped on the faces of the wounded in the wardroom below.

The wounded were taken down the hatch so quickly that the surgeon could do little more than tie up the bleeding arteries and attach a few splints to shattered limbs. There was no time for amputations – that would have to follow. Only when a leg or an arm hung by a shred did the ailing surgeon stop to sever it.

Nor was there any protection from the battle raging above. At least five cannonballs ripped through the walls of Parson's makeshift hospital. The doctor had just finished applying a tourniquet to the mangled arm of a young midshipman when a ball passed through the room and tore the boy out of the surgeon's arms, throwing him against the wall, his body half-severed. One seaman, brought down with both arms fractured, was scarcely in splints before another ball tore off his legs.

On the deck above, the carnage was dreadful as the

gun crews were felled by the British grapeshot. Perry called down through the skylight asking the surgeon to send up one of his assistants to man a gun. Every few minutes he called again, until there was no help left for the doctor.

Those who survived that battle would remember, years later, small bizarre incidents. At one point two cannonballs passed through the powder magazine – and didn't ignite it. Another entered the "light room" next to the magazine and knocked the snuff from a candle, but a gunner put it out with his fingers before the magazine could explode.

One shot punctured a pot of peas boiling on deck and scattered them. David Bunnell, working his gun, noticed a pig had got loose and was greedily eating the peas even though both its hind legs had been shot away.

Another shot struck a nearby gun, showering its crew with tiny pieces of gunmetal. One man was riddled from knees to chin with bits of cast iron, some as small as a pin-head, none larger than a buckshot. He recovered.

All the marines had been ordered down from the masts to replace the gunners. When the marines were put out of action, Perry called down the hatch, "Can any of the wounded pull a rope?"

Two or three managed to crawl on deck and lend a feeble hand. One of the sick men insisted on helping at the pumps so that the others could help with the guns. He was very ill and had to sit down to do the job. And at the end of the battle he was still sitting there, dead, a bullet through his heart.

The main battle took place between *Lawrence* on one side and the two largest British vessels – *Detroit* and *Queen Charlotte* – on the other. Elsewhere, things were going badly for the British. A cannonball carried away the rudder of *Lady Prevost*, one of the smaller British craft, and she drifted helplessly out of action. Her commander had been driven temporarily insane by a wound to his head. Another small British ship, *Little Belt*, lost her commander, ran to the head of the line, and was out of the fight.

But where was Jesse Elliott in the new brig *Niagara*? Perry's officers and men were in a fury to see that she was standing well off, using her long guns to little effect and too far out of range to bring her carronades into action. Elliott's

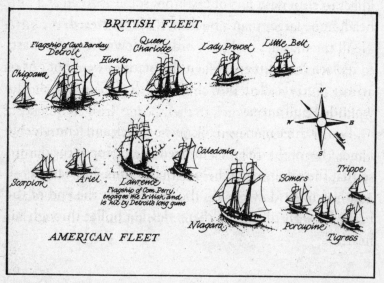

The Battle of Lake Erie: 12:15 p.m.

orders were to attack *Queen Charlotte*, which was hammering away at Perry's flagship. He had not done that. *Niagara* lurked behind the slower *Caledonia*, every spar in place, her crew scarcely scratched, her bulwarks unscarred.

Elliott and others had many explanations for this curious and dangerous lack of action, but none made any sense. In fact, it seemed that Elliott, angry at having been overtaken by a younger man and being removed from the lead at the last moment, was stubbornly following Perry's instructions (but only part of them) to stay at cable's length (182 m) from the vessel ahead. More than that, Elliott undoubtedly saw himself as the saviour of the day. When Perry was driven to surrender his flag, he, Elliott, would move in.

On *Lawrence*, even the wounded were cursing Elliott.

"Why don't they come and help us?" one seaman asked the bleeding Yarnell.

"We can expect nothing from that ship," came the bitter reply.

By two-thirty, Perry's flagship was in a shambles. Most of her guns were useless, smashed by the enemy's shot. A handful of gunners stuck to their posts, firing as quickly as they could. David Bunnell, in his haste, stuck a crowbar down the muzzle of his cannon and fired that, too. The gun grew so hot from constant use that it jumped from its carriage. By now five of Bunnell's crew of eight were casualties.

He moved to the next gun and, finding only one man

left, brought up his surviving crew members and tried to get that weapon into action. As he did, he looked down the deck and was shocked by what he saw: a tangle of bodies – some dead, some dying – the deck a welter of clotted blood, brains, human hair, and fragments of bones sticking to the rigging and planking. Of a hundred and thirty-seven officers and men aboard the flagship, only fifty-four had escaped injury or death.

One by one, *Lawrence*'s guns fell silent until she lay like a log in the water. Now another extraordinary event took place. Suddenly *Niagara* got under way. Apparently Elliott thought that Perry was dead. Now he took over, shouting an order to *Caledonia* directly ahead to move out of the line and let him pass – apparently to go to the aid of the disabled flagship. But he didn't do that. Instead he passed *Lawrence* on the windward side, leaving that vessel to the mercies of the British.

Aboard *Detroit*, Barclay, though badly wounded in the thigh, was secure in the belief that he had won the day. His ship, too, had taken a fearful pummelling. Its first officer was dead. Its spars and yards were shattered. Many of its guns were out of action. The deck was clear of corpses, however, for the British did not share the American reverence for the dead and threw all the bodies, except those of the officers, immediately overboard. Here, too, was one of the bizarre spectacles that highlighted this bizarre action – a pet bear, roaming the deck unhurt, licking up the blood.

But with Perry's flagship dead in the water, the wounded Barclay felt safe in his belief that the British had won a victory.

As it turned out, that was premature.

Chapter Seven

~

"We have met the enemy ..."

O LIVER HAZARD PERRY had no intention of giving up. Whatever motive Elliott had had for staying out of the battle, he had left Perry a seaworthy brig to continue the contest. And so Perry made a decision that would turn him into a national hero. He called for a boat, took four men, then turned to Yarnell.

"I leave you to surrender the vessel to the enemy," he said, and with that he ordered his men to pull for *Niagara*.

At the last moment he remembered his special flag and called for it. "If victory is to be gained, I'll gain it," he said.

He couldn't control his excitement. He refused to sit down until his men threatened to ship their oars because they feared for his life. The British, aboard *Detroit*, caught a glimpse of the little boat half-hidden by the gunsmoke. Musketballs whistled past Perry's head. Oars were shattered. Roundshot sent columns of spray into the boat. But Perry's Luck held. When a twenty-four-pound (11 kg) ball hit the side of the rowboat, he took off his jacket and plugged the hole.

Perry flees Lawrence for the ship Niagara.

On *Lawrence*, some of the wounded wanted to fight on instead of surrendering.

"Sink the ship!" they cried, and "Let us sink with her!"

But Yarnell did not intend to indulge in further sacrifice. As he reached *Niagara*, Perry turned and saw *Lawrence*'s flag come down. The British, however, couldn't board the prize – all of their lifeboats had been shattered.

Now the astonished Elliott saw the American commodore come over the side, a scarecrow figure, hatless, his clothes in tatters, blackened from head to foot by gunsmoke, spattered with blood.

"How goes the day?" asked Elliott needlessly.

"Bad enough," said Perry. "We have been cut all to pieces." Then: "Why are the gunboats so far behind?"

"I'll bring them up," said Elliott.

"Do so, sir," Perry replied shortly.

Elliott took a rowboat and started off through the heavy fire, using a speaking-trumpet to call the smaller craft forward into battle. He took command of the little *Somers*, and there he indulged in a strange display of temperament. When a cannonball whizzed across the deck he ducked and a gun captain laughed. In a fury Elliott struck him across the face with his trumpet and arrested the sailing master whom he believed to be drunk. But he got his gunboats quickly into action and poured a heavy fire on the British ships.

Perry was also in action. He hoisted his personal flag on *Niagara* and was intent on cutting directly through the

British line, dividing it in two. Barclay, who was back on deck with his wounds dressed, saw what Perry intended to do. A fresh breeze had sprung up. *Niagara* was bearing down at right angles to his ship. In a few minutes she'd be able to rake the full length of the British vessel with her broadside of ten guns. That was a manoeuvre that every commander feared.

Barclay knew what to do. He would have to bring his ship around before the wind so that his own broadside of undamaged guns could face *Niagara*. But before he could do that he was struck down again by a charge of grapeshot that tore his shoulder blade to pieces, leaving a gaping wound and rendering his one good arm useless. At the same

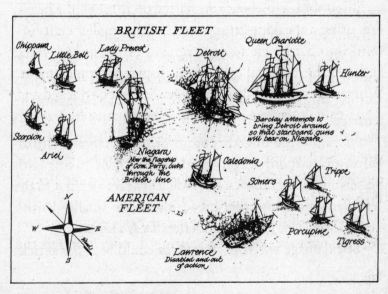

The Battle of Lake Erie: 2:40 p.m.

instant his second-in-command fell mortally wounded, and the ship was in charge of the young Lieutenant George Inglis.

Now the American gunboats in the stern began to rake the British vessels. Inglis tried to bring his badly mauled flagship around. But *Queen Charlotte*, which had been supporting Barclay in his battle with *Lawrence*, had moved in too close. She was lying directly astern in the lee of *Detroit*, which had literally taken the wind out of her sails.

Queen Charlotte's senior officers were dead. Robert Irvine had little experience in working a big ship under these conditions. As *Detroit* attempted to come around, the masts and the bowsprits of the two ships became hopelessly entangled and they were trapped. *Queen Charlotte* couldn't even fire at the enemy without hitting fellow Britons.

Only seven minutes had passed since Perry boarded *Niagara*. Now he was passing directly through the ragged British line, a half pistol-shot from the flagship.

"Take good aim, boys, don't waste your shot!" he shouted. His cannon were all double-shotted – two balls hurling through the air instead of one. That increased the carnage.

Niagara came directly abeam of the entangled British ships, and as it did so Perry fired his broadside, raking both vessels and also *Hunter*, which was a little bit astern. On the left, Perry fired his other broadside at two smaller British craft, *Chippawa* and the rudderless *Lady Prevost*.

The damage was frightful. Perry could hear the shrieks

of newly wounded men above the roar of the cannons. At this point every British commander and his second was a casualty and unable to remain on deck.

Looking across at the shattered *Lady Prevost*, Perry's gaze rested on an odd spectacle. Her commander, shot in the face by a musket ball, was the only man on deck, leaning on the companionway, his gaze fixed blankly on *Niagara*. His wounds had driven him out of his mind, and his crew, unable to face the fire, had fled below.

Detroit's masts crumbled under Perry's repeated broadsides. *Queen Charlotte's* mizzenmast was shot away. The ships were hopelessly entangled and taking a terrible beating. An officer appeared with a white handkerchief tied to

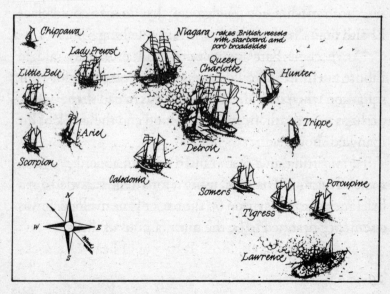

The Battle of Lake Erie: 3:00 p.m.

a pike. He couldn't haul down the flag because Barclay had nailed his colours to the mast.

Queen Charlotte, *Hunter*, and *Lady Prevost* all surrendered. Two British gunboats, *Chippawa* and *Little Belt*, attempted to make a run for it but were quickly caught. To Perry's joy, his old ship, *Lawrence*, drifting far astern, had once again raised her colours because the British had been unable to board her.

At three o'clock Perry's victory was absolute and unprecedented – the first time in history that an entire British fleet had been defeated and captured intact by its adversary. The ships built on the banks of the wilderness lake had served their purpose. They would not fight again.

When Elliott boarded *Detroit* there was so much blood on the deck that he slipped, drenching his clothing in gore. The ship's sides were studded with iron – roundshot, canister, and grapeshot – so much metal that no man could place a hand on its starboard side without touching some.

Down came Barclay's colours. And as Barclay said to Elliott, ruefully, "I would not have given sixpence for your squadron when I left the deck." He was in bad shape: weak, perhaps near death, from loss of blood and the shock of his mangled shoulder.

Perry, sitting on a dismounted cannon aboard *Niagara*, took off his round hat and, using it for a desk, scrawled out a brief message to Harrison on the back of an envelope. It was a sentence destined to be the most famous of the war:

"*We have met the enemy and they are ours. Two Ships, two Brigs, one Schooner, and one Sloop.*"

Around the lake the sounds of battle had been heard, but none could be sure who had won. At Amherstburg, Procter's deputy believed the British to be the victors. At Cleveland, seventy miles (112 km) away, a carpenter working on a new courthouse could hear the sound of the cannons. The villagers assembled to wait until the firing ceased. And because the last five reports came from heavy guns – American carronades – they concluded that Perry had won and gave three cheers.

Aboard *Lawrence*, as Perry returned to receive the official surrender, a handful of survivors greeted him silently. Twenty corpses lay on the deck, including close friends with whom he had dined the night before. He looked around for his little brother, Alexander, and found him sound asleep in a hammock, exhausted by the battle.

Perry put on his full-dress uniform, and received those members of the enemy still able to walk. They picked their way among the bodies and offered him their swords, which he refused to accept. Instead he inquired after Barclay. His concern for his vanquished enemy was real and sincere.

That night, as the September shadows lengthened, Perry lay down among the corpses, his fever having subsided under the adrenalin of battle. He folded his hands over his breast and, with his sword beside him, slept the sleep of the dead.

Chapter Eight

Aftermath

THE AMERICAN FLEET, with its prizes and its prisoners, was back at Put-in Bay by mid-morning on September 11. In the wardroom, Dr. Usher Parsons had been toiling since dawn amputating limbs. He had worked on ninety-six men and saved ninety-three.

A special service was held for the officers of both fleets. Barclay, in spite of his wounds, insisted on attending. Perry supported him, one arm around his shoulder. The effort was too much for the British commander, who had to be carried back to his berth on *Detroit*. Perry sat with him until the soft hours of the morning, when the British commander finally dropped off to sleep.

The prisoners were struck by the American's courtesy. Now that the heat of battle had passed, he looked on his foes without rancour, making sure his officers treated them well. To Barclay he was "a valiant and generous enemy."

The British commander would never again be able to raise his arm above his shoulder, and so he wrote to his fiancée offering to release her from their engagement. For once in his life, he was not "ill used." The spirited young woman replied that if there was enough of him left to contain his soul, she would marry him.

Elliott's behaviour had enraged Perry's officers. But Perry, intoxicated by victory, was in an expansive mood. He knew that Elliott had acted disgracefully, but he was too happy to take action against him. It was in his power to ruin Elliott's career, but that was not in his nature.

However, the contest between Perry and Elliott was not over. As the news of the great victory spread across the United States, as bonfires flared and public dinners, toasts, orations, songs, and poems trumpeted the country's triumph, the seeds of a bitter controversy began to sprout.

For the next thirty years, the Battle of Lake Erie would be fought again and again with affidavits, courts of inquiry, books, pamphlets, newspaper articles, even pistols. By 1818 Perry's own good nature had evaporated. He called Elliott "mean and despicable."

When Elliott challenged him to a duel, Perry responded by demanding his court-martial. It never took place. Even after Perry's death from yellow fever in 1819, the verbal war did not end: a literary battle went on. Nor did it die until the last of the participants had gone to their final rest to join those others, who, in the bloom of youth, had bloodied the raw new decks of two fleets that tore at each other on a cloudless September afternoon in 1813.

INDEX

ALCOHOL, 11

Alexander I, Tsar, 45

American fleet, 21, 25, 27, 34, 35-36, 42, 45-47, 54, 56-57, 74;
race to finish, 12, 13, 17, 22-23, 27;
superior firepower of, 39, 45-46;
superior manpower of, 47, 55;
victory of, 72-73

American troops, 10-11;
condition of, 11;
desertion of, 11;
from Kentucky, 10, 31, 39, 52;
numbers of, 34, 64;
Pennsylvania militia, 34;
readiness for battle of, 37;
reinforcements, 34, 37, 38, 39;
from Rhode Island, 52;
volunteers, 36-37

Amherstburg, 12, 38, 39, 44, 47, 73;
British shipbuilding at, 13, 21, 27, 28, 38

Austria, 45

BARCLAY, Captain Robert Heriot, 13-15, 18, 24, 25, 39, 42, 43, 44, 45, 47-48, 55, 64-65, 69, 72, 74-75;
career of, 18-19;
strategy of, 39-40, 42, 47, 54-55;
wounding of, 64, 69, 72

Battle rations, 11, 51-52

Black Rock, 23, 34

Bonaparte, Napoleon, 9, 45

Britain, and War of 1812, 9-10;
strategy, 25, 27;
troops, 10-11

British fleet, 19-21, 23, 25, 34, 36, 45-47, 51, 53;
race to finish building, 12, 13, 27-28;
superior long-range firepower of, 47, 55;
surrender of, 73

British troops:
British Right Division, 24;
condition of, 11;
desertion of, 11;